GW00570371

POOLS & GARDENS
PISCINES & JARDINS
POOLS & GÄRTEN

POOLS & GARDENS
PISCINES & JARDINS
POOLS & GÄRTEN

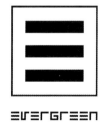

EVERGREEN

EVERGREEN is an imprint of

Taschen GmbH

© 2006 TASCHEN GmbH

Hohenzollernring 53, D-50672 Köln

www.taschen.com

Editor Editrice Redakteur:
Simone Schleifer

Editorial assistant Assistant d'édition Verlagsassistent:
Àlex Sánchez Vidiella

English translation Traduction anglaise Englische Übersetzung:
Scott Kleager

French translation Traduction française Französische Übersetzung:
Marion Westerhoff

Art director Direction artistique Art Direktor:
Mireia Casanovas Soley

Graphic design and layout Mise en page et maquette Graphische Gestaltung und Layout:
Oriol Serra Juncosa

Printed by Imprimé par Gedruckt durch:
Gráficas Toledo, Spain

ISBN-13: 978-3-8228-2791-8
ISBN-10: 3-8228-2791-6

Contents   Index   Inhalt

Human beings are enchanted by Nature. The feeling that links humans to the abundance of vegetation and to water in its multiple forms, such as fountains, lakes or rivers, causes them to constantly search for these elements in their urban surrounding, where concrete prevails. Hence, one of the biggest challenges architects and landscape designers are faced with is the integration of nature into their designs, via swimming pools and gardens, which provide man with memories of a paradise lost.

In the last few decades, and as a result of the increasing demographic growth, cities have gained space and have turned autochthonous flora and fauna into mortal victims of the urban sprawl. However, it is not easy to beat nature. As soon as traffic stops circulating, a motorway can be covered in weeds in no time. In Faust, Goethe described this force capable of filling the most inhospitable corners with life, as the "living mantle of divinity." Thanks to modern technology, architects today are able to exploit this natural force and satisfy even the most eccentric individual desires. Budget-permitting, they can create a rural oasis or even an ordered and minimalist Zen garden.

With continuous technological development, climate is no longer hampers set-up of pools and gardens. Although the innumerable advantages of choosing local vegetation, in terms of maintenance and care, are obvious, current humidity and temperature control systems make it possible to install a tropical garden in a Nordic area. On the other hand, the wide range of materials available nowadays means a swimming pool can be installed in excellent conditions. While plastic covers or metal and polyester pools are recommended in places with mild temperatures, stone and cement are suggested for extreme climates.

This book takes us around the world through swimming pools and gardens, divided into public and private facilities, with a comprehensive selection of new trends and the most contemporary designs of renowned architects and landscape designers.

L'être humain est fortement attiré par la nature : son besoin d'être en union avec la végétation exubérante et l'eau sous ses multiples formes –sources, lacs, fleuves—l'entraîne dans une quête constante des ces éléments au cœur de son environnement urbain, dominé par le gris du béton. De ce fait, l'un des plus grands défis à relever par les architectes et paysagistes est d'intégrer la nature dans leurs œuvres, par le biais de piscines et jardins qui rappellent à l'homme le paradis perdu.

Lors des dernières décennies, devant la croissance démographique constante, les villes se sont étendues au détriment de la flore et de la faune originelle, victimes de l'avancée de l'urbanisme. Mais, la nature ne se laisse pas vaincre facilement. Une autoroute abandonnée, est en peu de temps recouverte de mauvaises herbes. Goethe, dans son Faust, parle de cette force, capable de remplir de vie les recoins les plus inhospitaliers, comme « du manteau vivant de la divinité ». Aujourd'hui, grâce aux techniques modernes, les architectes disposent des moyens d'exprimer cette force naturelle et de satisfaire les désirs les plus extravagants de l'individu. En fonction du budget du client, tout leur est possible, de la conception d'une oasis bucolique à celle d'un jardin zen, bien agencé et minimaliste.

Grâce aux progrès constants de la technologie, les conditions climatologiques ne sont plus un frein à l'installation de piscines et jardins. Même s'il est évident que le choix d'une couverture végétale locale présente de multiples avantages sur le plan de la maintenance et de l'entretien, les systèmes actuels de réglage d'humidité et de température permettent d'installer un jardin tropical dans une zone nordique. D'un autre côté, le grand éventail de matériaux disponibles sur le marché actuel, permet d'installer une piscine dans d'excellentes conditions : les revêtements en plastique ou les bassins en polyester et métal sont recommandés dans les lieux aux températures clémentes, alors que dans les climats extrêmes, la pierre et le béton sont plus indiqués.

Ce livre, nous permet de musarder dans le monde des piscines et jardins, au gré d'une sélection divisée selon les installations publiques et privées, véritable panorama des nouvelles tendances et des designs les plus contemporains, œuvres d'architectes et de paysagistes à la renommée mondiale.

Der Mensch fühlt sich von der Natur sehr stark angezogen, seine Gefühle, die ihn mit der Üppigkeit der Vegetation und dem Wasser in verschiedenen Formen wie zum Beispiel Quellen, Seen oder Flüssen vereinen, führen ihn zu einer ständigen Suche nach diesen Elementen, auch in der städtischen Umgebung, die vom Grau des Betons beherrscht wird. Deshalb ist es eine der größten Herausforderungen für Architekten und Landschaftsplaner, die Natur mittels Pools und Gärten in ihr Werk aufzunehmen und so dem Menschen seine Erinnerung an das verlorene Paradies wieder zurückzugeben.

In den letzten Jahrzehnten wurden die Städte aufgrund des hohen Bevölkerungswachstums immer größer und die Flora und Fauna fiel diesem Fortschritt im Städtebau zum Opfer. Doch die Natur lässt sich nicht so leicht besiegen. Sogar eine Autobahn wird in kürzester Zeit von Unkraut bedeckt, wenn kein Verkehr mehr über sie hinweg rollt. Diese Kraft, jeden noch so ungeeigneten Fleck mit Leben zu erfüllen, wird in Goethes Werk Faust als „der Gottheit lebendiges Kleid" beschrieben. Heutzutage vermögen Architekten durch den Einsatz moderner Techniken diese natürliche Kraft zu akzentuieren und somit selbst den ausgefallendsten Wünschen gerecht zu werden. Ganz nach Geschmack und Budget des Kunden kann entweder eine idyllische Oase oder ein minimalistisch angeordneter Zen-Garten entworfen werden.

Dank des ständigen technologischen Fortschritts setzen selbst klimatische Faktoren der Gestaltung von Pools und Gärten nur bedingt Grenzen. Obwohl es selbstverständlich von Vorteil ist, einheimische Vegetation zu wählen, um die Pflege und Wartung zu vereinfachen, kann man jedoch mit den modernen Systemen zur Regulierung der Feuchtigkeit und Temperatur einen tropischen Garten in nördlichen Gefilden schaffen. Auch die große Materialauswahl auf dem Markt ermöglicht es, Pools zu konstruieren die den vorhandenen Gegebenheiten optimal angepasst sind. So sind widerstandsfähige Folien sowie vorgeformte Hartschalen aus Polyester oder Metall vor allem bei milden Temperaturen geeignet. Bei rauem Klima werden Materialien wie Stein oder Beton empfohlen.

Dieses Buch führt Sie durch die Welt der Pools und Gärten; unterteilt in private und öffentliche Anlagen. Es verschafft Ihnen einen umfassenden Überblick über neuste Tendenzen und modernste Designs, umgesetzt von weltweit anerkannten und renommierten Architekten und Landschaftsplanern.

Private Swimming Pools
Piscines privées
Private Pools

Water means life, recreation and a feast for the senses. No wonder more and more people want to have their own private oasis with a swimming pool.

The traditional swimming pool allows the bather to swim a few laps after a long day's work. However, a new design concept is becoming increasingly popular. Consisting of a smaller and more shallow surface area, it is conceived as a pool in which to take a comfortable seated bath. A pool design that is gaining in popularity has one or more of the pool edges covered by water, which creates a surface that resembles a frameless mirror. This effect is enhanced when the pool is above and in front of a larger body of water or built directly on a cliff. The impression of endless distances makes this kind of pool design one of the most popular.

Besides the rest and relaxation that a private swimming pool offers, air humidification and cooling systems are also important functions. When building a private swimming pool, for instance, designers often stress the importance of how close it is to the bordering living space, since the water of the pool can almost function as a natural air condition system.

The following chapter gives an overview of private swimming pool projects in various styles and concepts.

Eau est synonyme de vie, plaisir des sens et détente. Pour cette raison, de plus en plus de personnes recherchent leur oasis de tranquillité en construisant une piscine particulière.

La piscine traditionnelle permet au nageur de faire quelques brassées après une longue journée de travail. Toutefois, un nouveau concept de design fait de plus en plus d'adeptes. Il s'agit d'une surface plus petite et moins profonde destinée à prendre un bain, assis confortablement. Le design dont la cote de popularité monte en flèche est celui des piscines à débordement, où les bords de la piscine restent recouverts d'eau. Cette solution dote la piscine d'allures spectaculaires de miroir surdimensionné. L'effet est sublimé si la piscine se découpe devant un autre plan d'eau ou devant le vide d'une falaise. La sensation d'amplitude infinie fait que ce modèle est l'un des plus appréciés.

Outre leur fonction ludique, les piscines représentent un excellent système de réfrigération et de régulation de l'humidité. A cet effet, on les implante le plus près possible de l'espace intérieur habitable, afin de réduire la température ambiante en période de grosses chaleurs.

Ce chapitre offre divers projets qui donnent une vue d'ensemble des différents styles de conception de piscine privée.

Wasser ist gleichbedeutend mit Leben, Sinnesfreude und Erholung, und entsprechend legen sich immer mehr Menschen eine solche Oase der Erholung zu – einen privaten Pool.

Neben dem klassischen Pool, der vor allem für das „Erholungsschwimmen" nach einem langen Arbeitstag beliebt ist, finden zunehmend mehr auch diejenigen Modelle großen Zuspruch, deren Zugang zum Becken über eine breite Stufe erfolgt, auf der sich bequem sitzend oder liegend ein Bad unter freiem Himmel geniessen lässt. Eine weitere Form der Poolgestaltung stellen solche Anlagen dar, bei denen ein oder mehrere Beckenränder von Wasser bedeckt sind, und dadurch die Wasserobfläche, gleichsam wie ein ungerahmter Spiegel, eine beeindruckende Wirkung erzeugt. Neben der Entspannungs- und Erholungsfunktion privater Pools, ist auch die Bedeutung des Luftbefeuchtungs- und Kühlungssystems herauszustellen. So wird oftmals bei der Konstruktion privater Pools grosser Wert auf die Nähe zum angrenzenden Wohnraum gelegt, da hier das Wasser eine raumkühlende Funktion übernehemen kann. Im folgenden Kapitel werden Projekte vorgestellt, die einen Überblick über die unterschiedlichen Stile und Konzepte im Design privater Pools verschaffen.

House in the Mountains

Maison à la montagne

Haus in den Bergen

Surrounded by a hilly landscape, the hillside location of this residence offers the perfect panorama for the swimming pool.

Cette maison entourée de collines, perchée sur une falaise, offre un panorama idéal à savourer depuis la piscine.

Umrahmt von der hügeligen Landschaft, bietet die Hanglange dieser Residenz das perfekte Panorama für den Swimmingpool.

Tempate House

Maison Tempate

Tempate Haus

The aim of this design is to match manmade construction with the natural landscape all around.

Ce design a pour objectif de parvenir à un mimétisme entre l'oeuvre créé de la main de l'homme et le paysage naturel qui l'entoure.

Ziel dieser Gestaltung ist es, das Werk des Menschen in der umgebenden, natürlichen Landschaft nachzuahmen.

Pool in Malibu

Piscine à Malibu

Pool in Malibu

The breathtaking view that can be enjoyed from the terrace of this residence is enhanced by the location of its swimming pool, which faces the ocean.

Les vues impressionnantes, que l'on savoure depuis la terrasse de cette maison, sont sublimées par la piscine qui se découpe sur la mer.

Die beeindruckende Aussicht, die man von der Terrasse dieser Residenz aus geniessen kann, wird durch den zum Ozean hin ausgerichteten Swimmingpool noch verstärkt.

Bassil Residence

Résidence Bassil

Bassil Residenz

In designing this outer area with swimming pool, optical illusions were used to make the small area seem as large as possible.

L'altitude et l'emplacement de cet environnement splendide ont contribué à concevoir un univers qui parait spacieux malgré ses dimensions réduites.

Bei der Gestaltung dieses Aussenbereichs mit Swimmingpool wurde mit optischen Täuschungen gearbeitet, um den knappen Platz möglichst gross erscheinen zu lassen.

Residence in Pacific Heights
Résidence à Pacific Heights
Residenz in Pacific Heights

The organic, rounded structure that this swimming pool encloses strengthens its natural character and fuses it optically with the horizon.

La forme organique de cette piscine exalte son caractère naturel. De cet endroit, les vues sont exceptionnelles.

Die organische, abgerundete Struktur, die diesen Swimmingpool umschließt verstärkt den natürlichen Charakter und läßt ihn optisch Eins werden mit dem Horizont.

Elie Saab Residence

Résidence Elie Saab

Elie Saab Residenz

A consistent, rectangular design characterizes this garden, and is defined by the form of the pool and the arrangement of the stone slabs.

Un design particulièrement anguleux imprime le caractère de ce jardin déterminé par la forme de la piscine et la disposition des grandes dalles de pierre.

Ein konsequent verfolgtes, rechtwinkliges Design prägt diesen Garten und wird von der Form des Pools und der Anordnung der Steinplatten bestimmt.

Stiteler Residence

Résidence Stiteler

Stiteler Residenz

This pool rises almost like an oasis in the centre of extremely dry and arid surroundings.

Au coeur d'un environnement d'une aridité et d'une sécheresse extrêmes, la piscine s'ouvre à l'instar d'une oasis.

Inmitten einer extrem trockenen und dürren Umgebung erhebt sich dieser Pool nahezu wie einen Oase.

House in Tijucopava
Maison à Tijucopava
Haus in Tijucopava

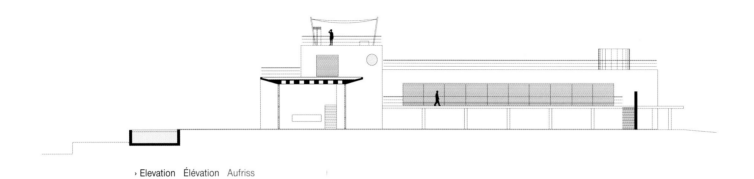

› Elevation Élévation Aufriss

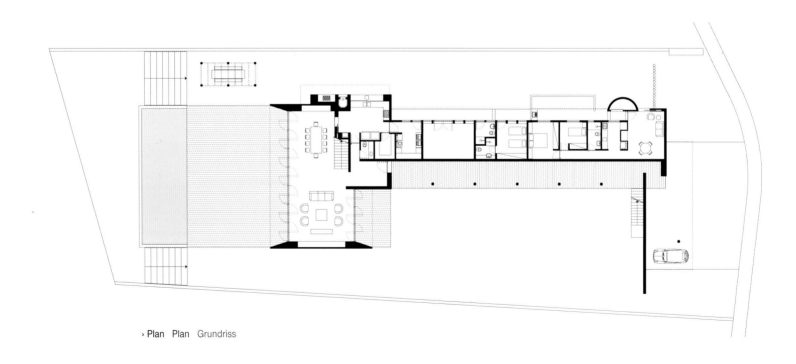

› Plan Plan Grundriss

Residence on the Coast

Résidence sur la côte

Residenz an der Küste

The interplay of contrasts is made evident on the outline of the pool, which is linear next to the house and wavy on the edge by the sea.

Le jeu de contrastes est visible sur les contours dessinés par la piscine : arrondis à côté de l'habitation et linéaires pour le bord qui donne sur la mer.

Das Spiel mit den Kontrasten wird besonders am Rand des Swimmingpools deutlich, am Haus ist er gerade und an der Seite, die zum Meer hin liegt, gewellt.

Maturucco Garden

Jardin Maturucco

Maturucco Garten

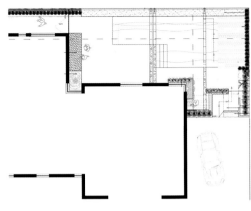

› Plan   Plan   Grundriss

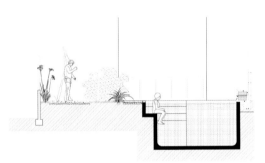

› Elevation   Élévation   Aufriss

The swimming pool – undoubtedly the star of this garden – is designed to take full advantage of the pleasure provided by the water.

La piscine, protagoniste indéniable de ce jardin, est conçue pour savourer les plaisirs de l'eau.

Der Swimmingpool hat ohne Zweifel die Hauptrolle in diesem Garten inne, der so entworfen wurde, dass man das Wasser genießen kann.

Yoder Residence

Résidence Yoder

Yoder Residenz

The architect designed this building with a large outer area, a reference to the concepts of modern masters like Mies van der Rohe, Wright and Schindler.

La conception de cet espace extérieur s'inspire des grands maîtres de l'architecture moderne, à l'instar de Mies van der Rohe, Wright et Schindler.

Der Architekt konstruierte dieses Gebäude in Anlehnungen an die Konzepte der grossen Meister der Moderne wie Mies van der Rohe, Wright und Schindler.

Residence in Mount Lebanon
Résidence à Mount Lebanon
Residenz in Mount Lebanon

A row of underwater lights marks the border between the areas of greater and lesser depth.

Une ligne de spots lumineux immergés affiche la limite entre le petit et le grand bain.

Eine Reihe kleiner, von Wasser bedeckter Strahler begrenzt visuell die unterschiedlichen Beckentiefen.

Tapada House
Maison Tapada
Tapada Haus

Wood is the material most used in the design of this terrace garden and it harmonizes nicely with the façade panelling.

Le bois, matière dominante sur cette terrasse paysagée, s'harmonise à merveille avec le revêtement de la façade de la maison.

Holz ist das am meissten verwendete Material bei der Gestaltung dieses Terrassengartens und passt sich harmonisch der Fassadenverkleidung des Hauses an.

Residence in Sitges
Résidence à Sitges
Residenz in Sitges

House in Florida

Maison en Floride

Haus in Florida

House in Miami Beach

Maison à Miami Beach

Haus in Miami Beach

Via a small footbridge, that also serves as a landing stage, this garden can be reached directly by boat.

On accède en canot à ce petit jardin, situé sur un petit débarcadère.

Über einen kleinen Steg, der als Anlegestelle dient, ist dieser Garten direkt mit dem Boot zu erreichen.

Minimalist Garden

Jardin minimaliste

Minimalistischer Garten

Dark, vertically placed wooden slabs serve as a screen and harmonize nicely with the earth tones of the vegetation.

Les planches verticales de bois foncé protègent des regards indiscrets tout en s'intégrant harmonieusement aux tons couleur de terre de la végétation.

Vertikal verlaufende, dunkle Holzplatten dienen als Sichtschutz und harmonieren zugleich mit den erdigen Tönen der Pflanzenwelt.

Sugerman House

Maison Sugerman

Sugerman Haus

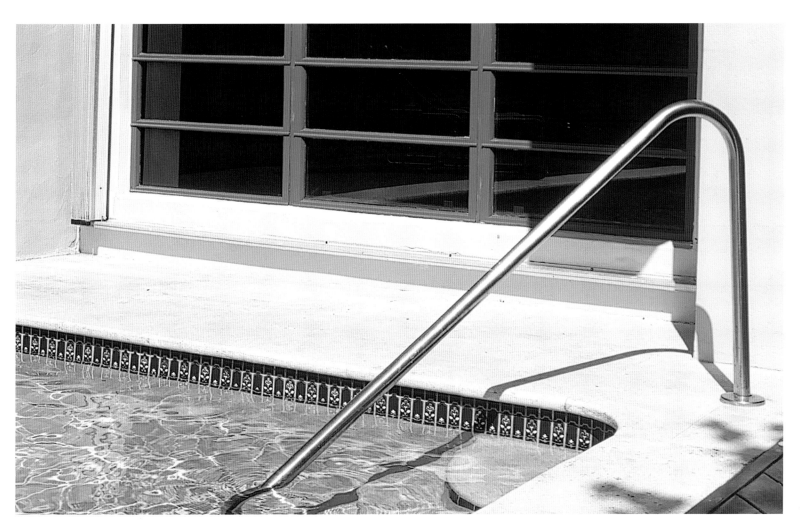

A humidifying system mounted to the house façade spays small jets of water into the swimming pool, which creates special ventilation and cooling.

Un système de régulation de l'humidité installé sur la façade fait gicler l'eau sur la piscine pour tempérer le climat.

Ein an der Hausfassade montiertes Befeuchtungssystem läßt kleine Wasserstrahle in den Pool spritzen und schafft somit besondere Kühlung und Belüftung.

Greenwald House

Maison Greenwald

Greenwald Haus

Angular forms and pale colors reign over both the garden and the house. Overall, the dominant tone is one of sobriety.

Les formes angulaires et les tonalités claires dominent tant dans le jardin que dans l'habitation. L'ensemble est emprunt de sobriété.

Die eckigen Formen und hellen Töne beherrschen sowohl den Garten als auch das Haus. So wirkt das Gesamtbild sachlich und schlicht.

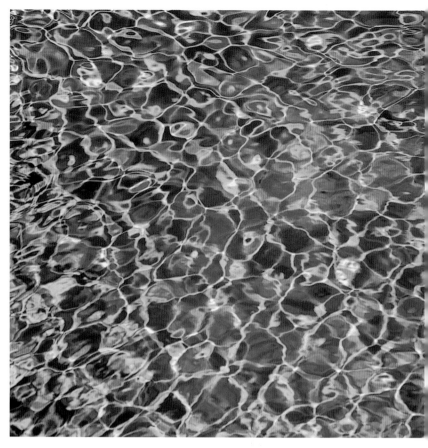

Palomares Residence

Résidence Palomares

Palomares Residenz

From the small pavilion you have a direct view of the pool and at the same time can enjoy the fresh, cool air generated by the water.

De la petite tonnelle, on aperçoit la piscine en savourant l'air frais généré par l'eau.

Von dem kleinen Pavillon aus kann man direkt auf den Pool blicken und zugleich von der frischen, kühlen Luft profitieren, die durch das Wasser generiert wird.

Chester House

Maison Chester

Chester Haus

Contrast played a role in the design of this garden: the clearly defined shape of the pool makes an even stronger impression next to the untamed growth of the vegetation.

Le design de ce jardin flirte avec le jeu de contrastes : la piscine anguleuse et clairement délimitée se détache de la flore sauvage.

Bei der Gestaltung dieses Gartens wurde mit Kontrasten gespielt und so wirkt der klarbegrenzte, rechtwinklige Pool noch stärker neben der wildwuchernden Pflanzenwelt.

Key Biscayne Residence

Résidence à Key Biscayne

Key Biscayne Residenz

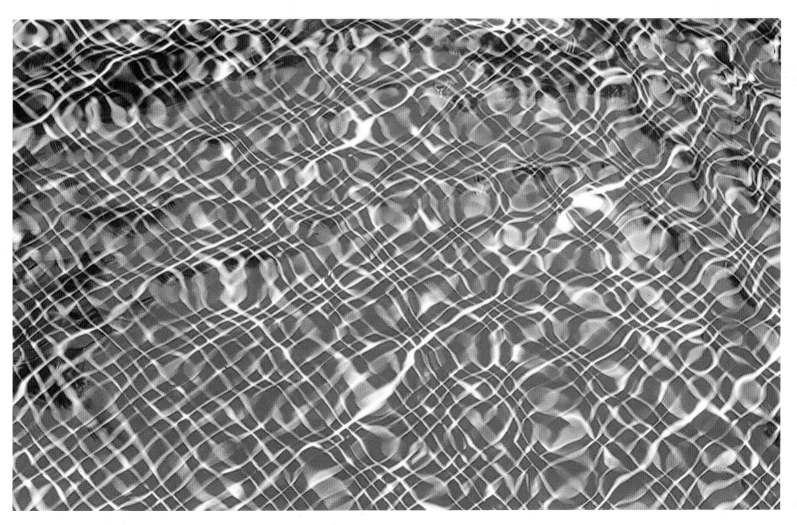

The black tiles give this swimming pool a unique character and communicate the impression of depth.

Le bleu marine de la grésite de la piscine accentue la sensation de profondeur.

Die dunkelblauen Kacheln verleihen dem Schwimmbecken einen individuellen Charakter und vermitteln den Eindruck von beachtlicher Tiefe.

House in Panzano
Maison à Panzano
Haus in Panzano

The rural and untouched surroundings inspired the architect here to a rustic design that is characterized by a liberal use of natural stone.

Cet environnement naturel a inspiré l'architecte dans la conception de ce design rustique défini par un usage soutenu de la pierre.

Die ländliche, unberührte Umgebung inspirierte den Architekt zu einem rustikalen Design, das von der Verwendung von reichlich Naturstein gekennzeichnet ist.

Private Pool

Piscine privée

Privater Pool

The defining characteristic of this garden is the meticulous distribution of its areas, which are clearly separated by means of materials and colors.

Ce jardin affiche une distribution parfaite en zones clairement délimitées par le biais de matériaux et couleurs.

Dieser Garten ist durch die Aufteilung in verschiedene Zonen gekennzeichnet, die deutlich durch Materialien und Farben voneinander getrennt sind.

Tropical Garden

Jardin tropical

Tropischer Garten

A true oasis of calm, this garden of palms, which takes up the aesthetics of the houses – wood and white.

Ce jardin, à la végétation tropicale, est une véritable oasis de paix en harmonie avec l'esthétique de la maison, qui conjugue blanc chaulé et bois.

Eine wahre Oase der Ruhe ist dieser Palmengarten, der die Ästhetik des Hauses – Holz und Weiß – wieder aufgreift.

Attic with Pool

Attique avec piscine

Dachgeschoss mit Pool

On the terrace on the roof of this building you can go for a swim while enjoying a view of the entire city.

La terrasse sur le toit de cet édifice offre un bain rafraîchissant ainsi qu'une vue splendide sur la ligne d'horizon de la ville.

Von der Dachterrasse dieses Gebäudes aus kann man die ganze Stadt überblicken und gleichzeitig ein erfrischendes Bad geniessen.

House in Arizona

Maison en Arizona

Haus in Arizona

The large dimensions of the elements that share this space bestow a touch of majesty on a setting in which time passes extremely slowly.

Les grandes dimensions des éléments, qui partagent cet espace, créent une ambiance tout en majesté, où le temps passe avec une lenteur extrême.

Die großen Elemente, die hier kombiniert werden, lassen eine majestätische Umgebung entstehen, in der die Zeit nur sehr langsam zu vergehen scheint.

Playa Langosta, Costa Rica | Juan Roca Vallejo, Abraham Valenzuela

Villa Marrakech

An elegantly designed garden in Moroccan style contains a T-shaped pool that opens directly onto a sandy beach.

Un élégant jardin de style arabe accueille une piscine en forme de T protégée par un jardin bucolique doté de palmiers.

Ein elegant gestalteter Garten im marokkanischen Stil, beherbergt den T-förmigen Pool, der direkt auf einen Sandstrand mündet.

House in Nosara

Maison à Nosara

Haus in Nosara

This pool required a complex structure in order to adapt it to the steep hillside location of the property.

La forme et situation de cette piscine ont dû surmonter les difficultés de construction sur un terrain à forte pente.

Aufgrund der steilen Hanglage des Grundstücks, musste dieser Pool in eine komplexe Struktur gefasst werden, um ihn den schwierigen Gegebenheiten anzupassen.

Jalan Ampang

The architect decided to build this pool on the roof of the house to take full advantage of the fascinating view and the light.

Pour profiter au maximum des vues fascinantes, l'architecte décide d'implanter la piscine sur la terrasse de toit de l'habitation.

Um die faszinierende Aussicht sowie das Licht voll auszuschöpfen, entschied sich der Architekt den Pool auf dem Hausdach anzulegen.

Los Sueños Residence

Résidence Los Sueños

Residenz Los Sueños

The effect of the tropical climate can be seen in the luxuriance of the vegetation in this recreation area.

L'incidence du climat tropical transparaît dans l'exubérance de la végétation de cette zone de repos.

Das tropische Klima lässt eine üppige Vegetation um diesen Ruhebereich wachsen und gedeihen.

Private Gardens

Jardins privés

Private Gärten

The term private garden encompasses a wide range of gardens, from the classic yard with a lawn at ground level to roof gardens, inner courtyards in the city, winter gardens, all the way to terrace gardens. Within this wide spectrum of private garden types, there are projects with vegetation that are covered in natural stone or concrete, or covered with wooden slabs. All private gardens, however, have one thing in common: they are an extension of living space and serve as a place of rest and relaxation. For this reason, private gardens should be tailored to the individual needs of home owners.

The quality of a particular garden will be determined by the distinctiveness of its design attributes. In this, fountains or springs, different materials, colours and special light effects can play an important role, and be supplemented by garden furniture that is both flexible and aesthetically pleasing.

The conception of a private garden, however, should not only be determined by aesthetic components. Besides considering the local weather conditions, designers have to consider the make up of the soil at that location as well.

This chapter presents examples of how wonderful paradises can be created in spaces that are often quite small.

Aujourd'hui, la notion de jardin privé abrite un concept très large qui englobe à la fois le tapis de gazon classique autour d'une habitation, les patios d'hivers et urbains ou les terrasses paysagées. Les idées de décoration de ces espaces marient zones vertes à revêtement de pierre, de dalles ou de bois. Mais, l'objectif est le même : agrandir l'espace habitable pour en faire un lieu de repos et de détente. Un jardin doit donc être réalisé en fonction des besoins individuels de ses propriétaires.

La qualité d'un jardin dépend, en dernier lieu, de ses attributs décoratifs. Et c'est là où entrent en jeu, jets d'eau et fontaines, gamme chromatique, éventail de matériaux et jeux de lumières. Pour parachever le tableau, il convient d'ajouter un mobilier adapté au jardin, polyvalent et esthétique à la fois.

Mais la conception du jardin ne doit pas s'arrêter uniquement aux considérations esthétiques. Il est indispensable de tenir compte des conditions locales du milieu ambiant et de la qualité du sol existant.

Ce chapitre offre plusieurs exemples de conversion de petits espaces en de véritables paradis.

Die Definition privater Gärten ist weit gefasst. Sie reicht von den klassischen Gärten, die ebenerdig angelegt und direkt vom Haus aus begehbar sind, über Dachgärten, städtische Innenhöfe und Wintergärten, bis hin zu Terrassengärten. Hierbei gibt es wiederum Projekte die begrünt sind, mit Naturstein oder Beton gepflastert oder mit Holzplatten bedeckt sind. Was allen Gärten jedoch gemeinsam ist: sie dienen als Erweiterung des Wohnraums und als Ort der Entspannung und Erholung. Entsprechend sollte der Garten auf die individuellen Bedürfnisse der Hausbesitzer optimal zugeschnitten sein.

Die Qualität des Gartens wird letztlich durch die gestalterischen Besonderheiten bestimmt. Hier können Wasserspiele oder Brunnen, unterschiedliche Materialien, Farben und besondere Lichteffekte eine wichtige Rolle spielen; bereichert durch gartentaugliches, flexibles und zugleich geschmackvolles Mobiliar.

Die Konzeption der Gartenanlage sollte jedoch nicht nur durch ästhetische Komponenten bestimmt werden. Neben der Beachtung der lokalen Wetterbedingungen sind auch die Bodenverhältnisse zu berücksichtigen. In diesem Kapitel werden Beispiele gezeigt, wie auf oftmals kleinstem Raum großartige Paradiese entstehen können.

Residence in Zurich

Résidence à Zurich

Residenz in Zürich

Water, present in both the pond and the pool, stands out in this garden as a powerful stimulus to the senses.

La présence de l'eau, dans l'étang et la piscine de ce jardin, est un véritable plaisir pour les sens.

Das Element Wasser ist im Teich und im Swimmingpool zu finden und dient in diesem Garten dazu, die Sinne anzuregen.

Garden in California
Jardin en California
Garten in Kalifornien

Curving waterways and small fountains give this garden a playful, lively character.

L'eau en mouvement du ruisseau et des fontaines met de la vie dans ce jardin.

Verwinkelte Wasserläufe sowie kleine Brunnen verleihen diesem Garten eine verspielte, lebendige Note.

Mediterranean Garden

Jardin méditerranéen

Mediterraner Garten

This project achieves a perfect balance between outer and inner rooms, and the two areas merge seamlessly into one another.

Ce projet réussit à créer un équilibre parfait entre les espaces intérieurs et extérieurs qui affichent une communication fluide.

Bei diesem Projekt wurde ein perfektes Gleichgewicht zwischen Außen- und Innenraum geschaffen, und die Bereiche gehen fließend ineinander über.

Asensio House

Maison Asensio

Asensio Haus

This garden, which was conceived as an area for solitude and silence, follows the clear design and minimalist line of the house.

Ce jardin est conçu comme zone de repos, selon un design précis aux lignes minimalistes.

Dieser Garten wurde als Ruhebereich konzipiert, der dem klaren Design und der minimalistischen Linie des Hauses folgt.

Kensington Garden

Jardin Kensington

Kensington Garten

Stone, wood, cypresses, yams and water converge in this garden, which has been carefully designed to satisfy the desires of its owners.

Pierre, bois, cyprès, yuccas et eau s'unissent dans ce jardin ingénieusement conçu pour le plaisir de ses propriétaires.

Stein, Holz, Zypressen, Yuccas und Wasser fließen in diesem Garten zusammen, der sorgfältig geplant wurde, um seinen Eigentümern als Ort der Erholung zu dienen.

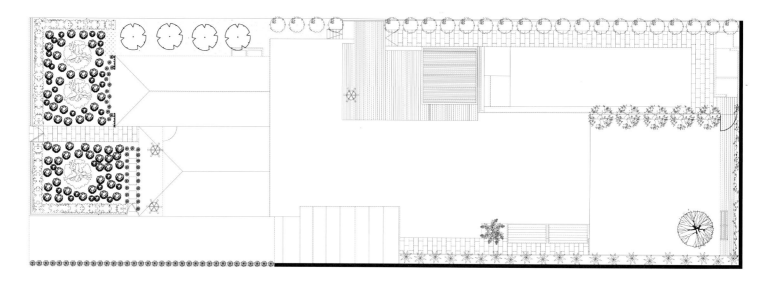

› Plan Plan Grundriss

Villa C

The aquatic plants that grow in the pond give it a rural feel.

Les plantes aquatiques qui poussent dans l'étang confèrent à ce jardin des allures champêtres.

Die Wasserpflanzen im Teich lassen diesen Garten sehr ländlich wirken.

Barcelona, Spain | Luisa Mellis, Marcos Basso Cano, Carmen Basso de Ros

Attic in Pedralbes

Attique à Pedralbes

Dachgeschoss in Pedralbes

A distinct design was conceived for each of this two exterior areas: grass combined with limestone on the rooftop, and teak alternating with white gravel on the terrace.

Le design est différente pour ces deux surfaces extérieures : association de gazon et de pierre calcaire sur le toit, alternance de bois de teck et de gravier blanc pour la terrasse.

Es wurden Formen der Gestaltung für die beiden Außenbereiche gefunden: Rasen in Kombination mit Kalkstein auf der Dachterrasse und Teakholz mit weißem Kies auf der Terrass

Tuin in Wollerau

Jardin à Wollerau

Garden in Wollerau

The grey tones of the concrete and the stone slabs lend this garden a minimalist character.

Les tons gris du béton et des dalles de pierre imprègnent ce jardin d'une note minimaliste.

Die Grautöne des Betons und der Steinplatten verleihen dem Gesamtbild dieses Gartens einen minimalistischen Charakter.

233

House in Palo Alto
Habitation à Palo Alto
Haus in Palo Alto

Garden in Winkel

Jardin à Winkel

Garten in Winkel

The basic idea for the design of this garden was to extend the living area to the outside and to make garden maintenance easy.

L'idée sous-jacente à la conception de ce jardin est d'accroître la superficie de la maison en l'ouvrant sur l'extérieur, avec des solutions évitant un entretien trop fastidieux.

Die Grundidee bei der Gestaltung dieses Gartens war es, eine Erweiterung des Wohnraums nach aussen zu schaffen, der gleichzeitig absolut pflegeleicht ist.

Ivy Street Roof Garden

Terrasse à Irvy Street

Dachterrasse in der Ivy Street

› Plan Plan Grundriss

Chromatic Play

Jeux de couleurs

Farbspiel

The designer of this house also lives here – the design of its garden is an interpretation of a journey through the desert.

Le designer et occupant de la maison dotée de ce jardin, l'a conçu à l'instar d'un voyage au désert.

Der Designer und selbst Bewohner des Hauses, das zu dem Garten gehört, interpretiert mit seinem Entwurf eine Reise durch die Wüste.

Sonoma Residence

Résidence Sonoma

Sonoma Residenz

he different zones of this public garden are distinguished from each other through the use of different plants.

e design soigné et original de la zone paysagée forme un vivant contraste avec la végétation sylvestre qui entoure la piscine.

ie unterschiedlichen Zonen dieses offenenen Gartens werden durch verschiedene Bepflanzungen voneinander differenziert.

Kaufmann House

Maison Kaufmann

Kaufmann Haus

The orthogonal shape of the house is broken by the sinuosity that distinguishes all the elements making up the garden.

La volumétrie orthogonale de la maison est brisée par la sinuosité de tous les éléments faisant partie du jardin.

Die rechtwinklige Form des Hauses wird durch die kurvigen Formen der Elemente, die zum Garten gehören, unterbrochen.

Bronx Garden

Jardin dans le Bronx

Bronx Garten

This rooftop covered with lush greenery becomes a pleasant refuge in the summer months.

Cette terrasse de toit, tapissée d'une abondante végétation, se transforme pendant les mois d'été en un véritable coin de paradis.

Diese Dachterrasse ist von üppiger Vegetation bedeckt und wird so in den Sommermonaten zu einem erholsamen Ort des Rückzugs.

Corso Garden
Jardin Corso
Corso Garten

The mirror placed at the back area of this garden is a unique way to create a sense of largeness, in that the green zone of the house is doubled.

L'idée ingénieuse d'installer un miroir de grandes dimensions au fond du jardin, confère à cet espace extérieur une agréable sensation de largesse.

Der im hinteren Bereich des Gartens platzierte Spiegel ist ein einzigartiges Mittel um Weite zu erzeugen, indem die Grünzone des Hauses verdoppelt wird.

Garden in Florida

Jardin en Floride

Garten in Florida

The profuse, leafy vegetation turns this garden into a cool refuge from the tropical climate of Florida.

La végétation exubérante et luxuriante transforme ce jardin en un lieu de fraîcheur où se protéger du climat tropical de Floride.

Die üppige und dichte Vegetation macht aus diesem Garten einen kühlen Ort, an dem man dem tropischen Klima Floridas entkommen kann.

Garden in La Jolla
Jardin à La Jolla
Garten in La Jolla

This garden, in which there is a small pavilion, creates a landscape that allows both meditation and the chance to enjoy nature.

Le jardin, et sa petite tonnelle, forment un lieu idéal pour méditer et savourer la nature.

Der Garten in dem sich ein kleiner Pavillon befindet, schafft eine Landschaft, die der Meditation und dem Naturgenuss dient.

Private Garden
Jardin privé
Privater Garten

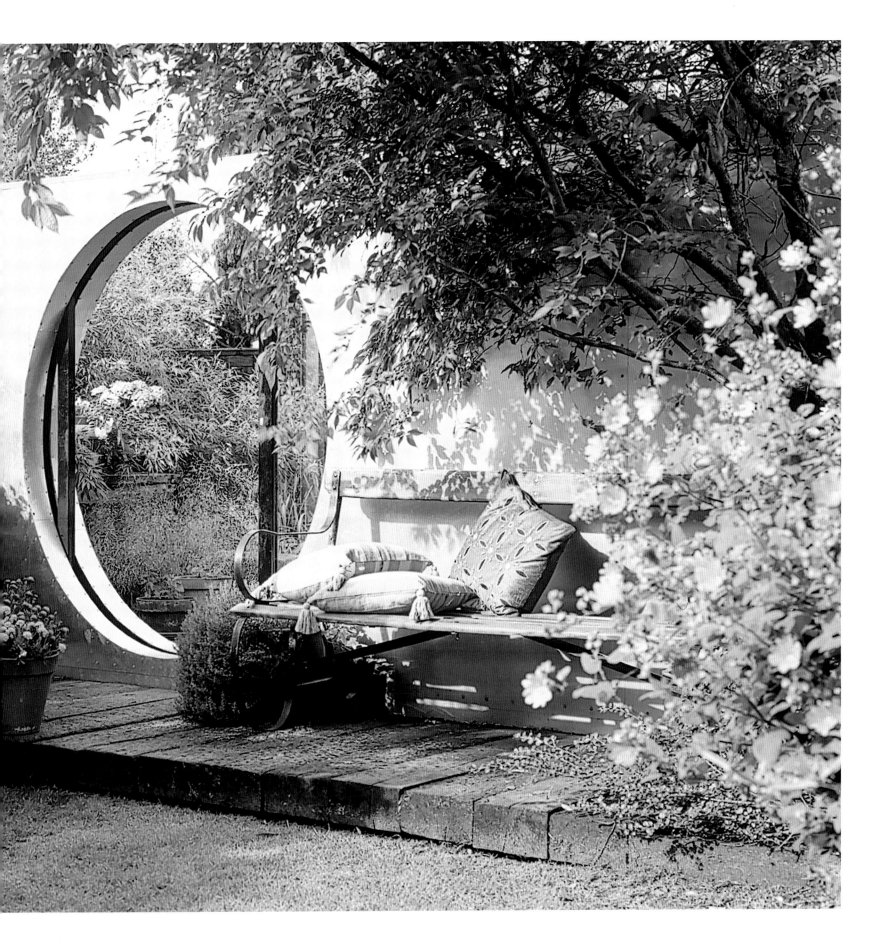

Public Gardens
Jardins publics
Öffentliche Gartenanlagen

During the last few years, an important change in landscape architecture has taken place regarding how landscapes are understood. What was once seen as work carried out parallel to that of architects and construction engineers, has since developed into a discipline in its own right, one in which the concepts of architecture, urban planning, biology and modern art are combined. Using unusual designs and projects, this section of the book will chronicle how, what used to be seen as design solutions of a mostly functional nature, have developed into predominantly aesthetic design solutions in which the influence of other cultures is unmistakable.

Besides the aesthetic aspects, the interaction between climate and vegetation has become an important factor in design as well. The goal of design can therefore be understood as achieving an optimal balance; where small ecological niches can exist on their own and can regenerate themselves with relatively little maintenance and care.

This chapter presents projects at various locations with unusual solutions under the most different of conditions.

Il s'est produit, ces dernières années, un changement radical dans la conception architecturale des paysages et l'approche de l'environnement naturel. Ce qui, autrefois, était une tâche accessoire pour les architectes et ingénieurs, est aujourd'hui une discipline à part entière, alliant architecture, urbanisme, biologie et art contemporain. Un rapide coup d'oeil sur les designs et projets des dernières décades permet de constater une nette évolution : les designs actuels sont en quête constante de solutions définies par l'aspect esthétique, où les touches multiculturelles sont les bienvenues.

Mais dans la conception d'un jardin, outre les aspects esthétiques, il est indispensable de prendre en compte la relation entre climat et végétation. Si certaines espèces s'adaptent aux conditions du milieu ambiant, elles modifient et régulent à leur tour le climat. Donc le but est de réussir un équilibre optimal pour que ces petits coins de verdure écologiques, survivent et se régénèrent avec un minimum de soin et d'entretien.

Ce chapitre réunit des projets situés à divers endroits, offrant des solutions originales aux conditions de milieu ambiant les plus variées.

In den letzten Jahren hat im Bereich der Landschaftsarchitektur ein bedeutender Wandel in der Auffassung stattgefunden, wie Landschaft verstanden und gestaltet wird. Was man früher als eine Arbeit verstand, die parallel von Architekten und Bauingenieuren durchgeführt wurde, hat sich zu einer eigenen Disziplin entwickelt, in welcher die Konzepte der Architektur, der Stadtgestaltung, der Biologie und der zeitgenössischen Kunst vereint wurden. Anhand ungewöhnlicher Entwürfe und Projekte wird eine Entwicklung aufgezeigt, bei der einem früher eher funktionellen Design, nunmehr überwiegend ästhetisch geprägte Ge-staltungslösungen entgegensetzt werden, wobei der Einfluss anderer Kulturen unverkennbar ist.

Neben dem ästhetischen Aspekt ist die bestehende Wechselbeziehung zwischen Klima und Vegetation ein wichtiger Faktor. Das Ziel der Gestaltung ist somit in der Schaffung eines optimalen Gleichgewichts zu sehen, derart, dass die kleinen ökologischen Nischen autonom bestehen und sich mit relativ geringem Aufwand an Wartung und Pflege selbst generieren können.

In diesem Kapitel werden Projekte an verschiedenen Standorten gezeigt, die ungewöhnliche Lösungen unter den unterschiedlichsten Bedigungen vorstellen.

Adelaide Street

To create a harmonious atmosphere with this small city garden, its design language and the choice of materials were adapted to the building.

Pour réaliser un environnement harmonieux dans ce petit jardin citadin, le langage formel et matériel est dans la veine de l'édifice.

Um eine harmonische Umgebung in diesem kleinen Stadtgarten zu schaffen, wurden die formale Sprache sowie die Materialauswahl der des Gebäudes angepasst.

Geneve, Switzerland | Jean-Michel Landecy, Nicolas Deville, Jean-Marc Anzévui

Louis-Jeantet Foundation Garden

Jardin de la Fondation Louis-Jeantet

Garten der Louis-Jeantet Foundation

This project consists of three central themes: renovation of the villa, the construction of an auditorium and the design of a garden that gives order to the whole.

Ce projet avait trois objectifs : la restauration du palais, la construction d'un auditorium et la conception d'un jardin qui harmonise le tout.

Dieses Projekt besteht aus drei zentralen Themen: die Renovierung der Villa, die Errichtung eines Auditoriums und der Entwurf eines Gartens, der das Gesamtbild gliedert.

Diagonal Mar Park

Parc de Diagonal-Mar

Diagonal Mar Park

This park is design from a central axis with paths that expand outward in various directions like the branches of a tree.

Le parc s'articule autour d'un axe central et divers sentiers qui s'étendent dans plusieurs directions, à l'image des branches d'arbre.

Der Park wird von einer zentralen Achse strukturiert, von der Wege, die sich in verschiedene Richtungen ausbreiten, wie Zweige eines Baumes abgehen.

Public Square
Place publique
Öffentlicher Platz

Elements like Roman ruins are displayed here under a glass cupola and surrounded by a modern, futuristic design.

Des éléments anciens, comme les ruines romaines, sont exposés sous ces coupoles de cristal, encadrés d'un design moderne et futuriste.

Antike Elemente wie Überrreste aus der Römerzeit werden unter den Glaskupeln ausgestellt und mit einem zeitgenössischen, futuristischen Design umrahmt.

General Mills Corporate

This parking area within a building complex offers rest and relaxation with a variety of seating possibilities.

La zone paysagée de ce complexe est un havre de paix et de repos pour ceux qui peuvent se permettre de faire une halte dans leur journée de travail.

Diese Parkanlage innerhalb eines Gebäudekomplexes bietet einen Ort der Ruhe und Entspannung mit einer Vielzahl an Sitzgelegenheiten.

Georg-Freundorfer-Plaza

This park, located in one of the most densely populated parts of the city, is used for leisure time activities, for relaxation and for going for walks.

Cette installation située dans la zone plus peuplée de la ville, offre un espace agréable pour développer les activités de loisir.

Diese Anlage in dem am dichtest bebauten Teil der Stadt, dient sowohl zum Nachgehen der Freizeitaktivitäten als auch zum einfachen Erholen und spazieren gehen.

VP Bank

On a paved area made of granite slabs is a large, rectangular flower tub; the basin stores water for the plants.

Les petits réservoirs rectangulaires qui parsèment la couverture végétale ont un but à la fois décoratif et fonctionnel : recueillir l'eau de pluie.

Auf einer Pflasterung aus Granitplatten steht ein großer rechteckiger Blumekübel; die Wasserbassins als Speicher für Gieswasser.

North Terrace Gardens

Jardins à North Terrace

North Terrace Gärten

This linear garden was designed to emphasize the civic and culture importance of North Terrace Boulevard.

Ce jardin linéaire est conçu pour accentuer le côté bourgeois et culturel de l'axe du North Terrace Boulevard.

Dieser lineare Garten wurde entworfen, um die Bedeutung der bürgerlichen und kulturellen Achse des North Terrace Boulevards zu unterstreichen.

Lurie Garden

Jardin Lurie

Lurie Garten

Several different symbolic elements were fused in this garden at the Lakefront Millennium Park, to erect a large recreational area.

Ce jardin du Lakefront Millennium Park intègre divers éléments allégoriques pour aménager un immense parc de loisirs.

Bei diesem Garten im Lakefront Millennium Park wurden verschiedene sinnbildliche Elemente zusammengeführt um eine große Freizeitanlage zu errichten.

348

Le Nouveau Jardin de la Bastide

A modular structure integrates the most important characteristics of the garden – exotic, ethno botanic, ecological and modern. It is the starting point of the garden's arrangement.

La structure modulaire de ce jardin botanique est le concept qui gère la distribution de l'ensemble de l'espace.

Eine modulare Struktur fasst die wichtigsten Eigenschaften des Gartens und ist Ausgangspunkt der Komposition des Gartens.

Charlotte Garden

Jardin Charlotte

Charlotte Garten

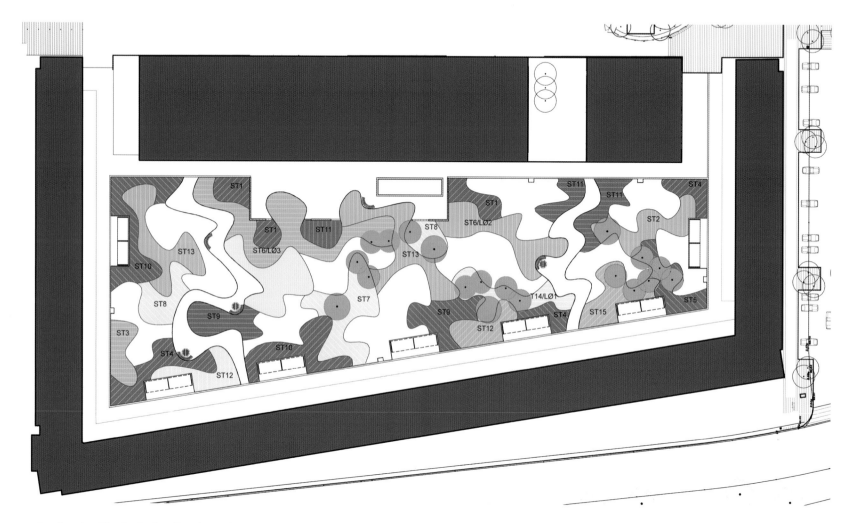

› Location plan   Plan de situation   Umgebungsplan

This garden is a new interpretation of the traditional northern European garden. Though located in the middle of a block of houses, it feels open and large.

Cet espace réinterprète les zones vertes traditionnelles de l'Europe du nord : tout en étant situé dans un patio planté de pommiers, il est ample et dégagé.

Diese Gartenanlage ist eine Neuinterpretation der traditionellen Gärten Nordeuropas. Er befindet sich im Zentrum eines Häuserblocks, wirkt jedoch offen und weit.

Grindaker

Water Park

Parc de l'Eau

Wasserpark

Water is the central design element of this park, in the form of large basins, waterways and fountains.

L'eau est l'élément clé du design de ce parc, et se présente sous forme de grands bassins, canaux et jets d'eau.

Wasser ist das Hauptelement bei der Gestaltung dieses Parks und wurde in Form von großen Becken, Wasserläufen und Springbrunnen angelegt.

Town Hall Square

Place de la Mairie

Rathausplatz

Circular shapes characterize the design of this park in the middle of a city and they brake up the square geometry of the blocks of houses in a playful way.

Les formes circulaires déterminent la conception de ce parc au coeur de la ville et reposent de la symétrie angulaire des édifices

Kreisformen bestimmen das Bild bei der Gestaltung dieses Parks inmitten der Stadt und lockern die rechtwinklige Geometrie der Häuserblocks auf spielerische Weise auf.

Forest Gallery

A large courtyard in the Melbourne Museum is home to the Forest Gallery, a faithful reproduction of the Tall Forests area to the east of the city.

Le grand patio du Musée de Melbourne s'ouvre sur la Forest Gallery, fidèle reproduction de la zone Tall Forests, située à l'est de la ville.

In dem großen Hof des Museums von Melbourne befindet sich die Forest Gallery, eine originalgetreue Nachbildung einer Zone der Tall Forests, der sich östlich der Stadt befinden.

Photo Credits Crédits photographiques Fotonachweis